# Daily Hope
## for Today's
## Christian Woman
### Devotional

Dr. Bukky Ojuola

ISBN 978-1-63844-444-2 (paperback)
ISBN 978-1-63844-445-9 (digital)

Christian Faith Publishing, Inc.
832 Park Avenue
Meadville, PA 16335
www.christianfaithpublishing.com

Printed in the United States of America

A thirty day devotional for today's Christian woman who is excited to learn that victory is attainable through a personal relationship with Jesus Christ. Be encouraged by each woman's story, and allow it to inspire you to develop into the unique masterpiece that God designed and handcrafted.

# The Woman at the Well

John 4:5–29

"Come and see a Man who told me all things that I ever did."

The Samaritan woman could boast about her knowledge of men. She had a history with men because she had five failed attempts at marriage and was currently living with a man that she was not married to. She had learned, by experience, that men could not be trusted. Through the past broken relationships, she had endured many disappointments—being lied to, used, dumped, flattered but not loved, loved but not kept. She discovered that she was not worth fighting for, by at least five men that she had given her heart to.

She had given up on finding true unconditional love and acceptance. She had settled for the current arrangement she had with her boyfriend. However, her life story dramatically changed when she met Jesus at the well. He was *her seventh man*, but she quickly realized that He was totally different from any other man she had ever met. Even though He told her *everything she ever did*, He did not pass judgment on her and did not drop her like the others had done.

Jesus offered her more than He was asking of her. He was reliable, and He was there for her—waiting at their original meeting place. He offered her the hope that no man had ever given, assured her of a better future, provided her a promise of lasting joy. Her encounter with Jesus ended her search for love—she had found the man that she could be vulnerable with, pour out her love upon, and trust with all her life—past, present, and future.

If you are tired of searching for love and burnt too many times by relationships that drained rather than built you up, you too can put an end to your search for a mystical Prince Charming. Today, let Jesus have your past and present and trust your future to Him. He is the ONLY one who has promised NEVER to leave you nor forsake you. No matter what disappointments you have faced, He is able and willing to start over with you wherever you are. He is the God of all hope, and He can be trusted (Rom. 15:13).

## Personal Reflections/Notes

_____
_____
_____
_____
_____
_____
_____

## Action Steps

_____
_____
_____
_____
_____
_____
_____

# Mary Magdalene

—— ✿ ——

## Luke 8:1, 2; Matthew 27:56, 61; Matthew 28:1, 5–8; John 20:11–13, 16–18

Mary Magdalene had come to accept the oppression and darkness that came from her demons. She had resigned to a life of fear, anxiety, depression, and repression. She had given up all hope of ever living without hearing those tormenting voices all day. She felt totally helpless, unable to get free no matter what she did or who tried to help her. She had lost her own voice and only spoke out whatever was whispered to or yelled at her. They spoke, she obeyed. She had become so accustomed to the voice of terror and torment that she could not bear to be alone. Truly, she was never alone because her demons never left her without company (albeit unwanted). She had come to accept her life of bondage and harassment until she met the ONE who made her demons tremble and flee in terror, the Man who gave her freedom from her terrorizers and tormentors.

Jesus restored meaning and a sense of purpose to Mary's life. He gave her value and restored her hope completely. She walked with Him until she knew His voice. She came to discover the reason for her existence: to announce the resurrection of her Savior to the world! Her life went from one of despair and purposelessness to one that was fulfilled with a newfound exuberance as she learned not to be afraid of being alone. She now relished the quiet, solitary moments with her Lord, longing to meet Him in the garden. Fear was gone; shame and regret had died. She was free to live and daily proclaim the hope of an eternity with a resurrected Lord!

You might have been plagued in your mind with hallucinations, anxiety, and depression and lost all hope of ever living a productive life without medications or other treatment. Thankfully, God is no respecter of persons (Acts 10:34; Rom. 2:11). If He got Mary Magdalene free, He will do the same for you as long as you hold on to His word and trust Him to get you absolutely free.

## Personal Reflections/Notes

_____

_____

_____

_____

_____

_____

_____

## Action Steps

_____

_____

_____

_____

_____

_____

# The Woman Caught in Adultery

—— ⸉⸎ ——

## John 8:1–11

### Taken in adultery, in the very act.

She was condemned and deserving of death because she had violated the commandment "thou shall not commit adultery." Her man never came to her rescue. Even though he had told her how much he loved and valued her. Now she was facing death all alone—abandoned, ashamed, confused, and totally lost. She fell from a height of ecstasy to the lowest depth of despair. Her well-kept secret has now become headline news in the community. Her condemnation was sure. There was no escaping death by stoning for such an abominable offense. She could see the finality in the eyes of her accusers, who each had a deathly stone that will seal her destiny forever.

Her whole life played before her eyes, and suddenly, her eternity seemed very uncertain and bleak. At an unusual turn of events, her accusers decided to talk to a man who would decide her fate. When she opened her eyes, she saw the most compassionate man she had ever met. He surely was different from her guy, who is now nowhere to be found. Nevertheless, this man is a rabbi, a teacher of the Law, and would surely condemn her according to the Law. He certainly would not violate the Law in any way. So either way, His verdict would be the same: "death by stoning."

Her shame and guilt kept her head down. One after another, she began to see individual stones pile up beside her instead of on top of her. Soon enough, she realized there was not one of her accusers left. All of them had quietly left, with their weapons of destruction left behind. Now it was just her and Jesus. That was when she realized she had been translated from death to life. He had come to her rescue and freed her with His words, "neither do I condemn you, go and sin no more." The words rang deep in her heart, shook her very core. She received undeserved mercy for a judgment she so deserved.

What does that even mean? Freedom, a clean slate, new beginning, fresh start, recovery—all of these and much more! She got another chance; she received mercy from the Lord of mercy, who freed her with those ten words. His words brought life and not death, mercy and not judgment, hope in place of defeat. She was empowered to proclaim, confidently and in total humility, the undeserving and unmerited mercy she had just received. Do you feel like you have blown all your chances, taken too many wrong turns, committed the unpardonable sin, and therefore undeserving of mercy? Will you take God at His word and let Him free you of every chain from your past? He's saying to you, today, in the presence of your accuser, Satan, "neither do I condemn you, go and sin no more."

## Personal Reflections/Notes

_____

_____

_____

_____

_____

_____

## Action Steps

_____

_____

_____

_____

_____

_____

# Woman with the Issue of Blood

———— ⌒❧⌒ ————

## Luke 8:43–48; Matthew 9:20–22; Mark 5:25–34

> She had suffered much from many doctors,
> had become poor, and was no better but worse.
>
> —Mark 5:26 TLB

This woman was spent, weakened, stripped of every dignity, resource, hope, and life purpose. She was told, "There's nothing else we can do for you." It was over, too late for her, and she could not recover from the disease or damage, according to many doctors' reports. Death was upon her, and she could not fight anymore. Until she heard of the healing Jesus, and He was coming her way! She determined to sneak up and touch His garment in faith that she will be made whole. She was going to put all she had into this one touch, believing for a miracle. It would be the touch of a lifetime. She was not even bold enough to go and talk to Him. Without informed consent, and taking matters into her own hands, she secretly reached out and touched Him.

Instantly, she knew she was healed—that sick feeling that she had become so accustomed to was no longer there. She had vigor and vitality. She had a surge of divine power and strength go through her entire being, and immediately, she was made whole. She received her healing and restoration without paying a dime, without signing pages upon pages, not another *informed consent* or procedure needed.

She had encountered the one physician who could heal without surgery and restore without complications or side effects.

You might have been bruised and battered, left without hope of a cure, a failed experiment, left to pine away. The experts and top medical scientists might have told you, "There's nothing else we can do for you." All hope is not lost because there's the Master Physician who's making His rounds, and He has you on His mind. You don't need anyone's permission—not your doctor, family, pastor, friends—to reach out to Jesus, the Great Physician. He takes people without insurance, referrals, co-pay, and all the red tape you know too well. He won't cast you away nor rebuke you for sneaking up. He's more than willing to heal (Matt. 8:3), especially you. This is your moment, seize it—be healed and made whole, in Jesus's name!

Additional resources on healing (scriptures related to healing): Phil. 1:6; John 10:10; Psalm 103:2–5; Isa. 53:4, 5; Prov. 4:20–22; Psalm 91:9, 10, 14–16; 2 Tim. 1:7; Isa. 40:29, 31, 2; Phil. 4:6, 7.

## Personal Reflections/Notes

_____

_____

_____

_____

_____

_____

_____

## Action Steps

_____

_____

_____

_____

_____

_____

_____

# The Widow of Nain

———— ❦ ————

## Luke 7:11–15

Loss. Another one has been taken, stolen before she had a chance to do anything. She had been robbed again. This woman had become acquainted with grief and loss. First, it was the death of her husband—the man of her dreams whom she had hoped to grow old with. Now, her only son had just died. What else could be taken away? She couldn't get rid of that hollow sense of desolation that filled her inner being. Her tears overflowed from the depths of emptiness, from a dry well because she was now totally spent. No one could truly console this woman; no words could reach the depth of her pain. Her family, friends, neighbors tried all they could, but what do you say to fill such a void? Her past was already taken with her husband's untimely death. Now, her future was stolen with her son's passing. All her hope vaporized into thin air, slipping right through her fingers.

It appeared like the enemy had gotten away with stealing from her again. She thought to herself; *All hope is lost.* But thank God the funeral procession ran into the resurrection and life! His compassion moved Him to act on her behalf. He not only comforted her with His kind words, "Don't cry," He restored her future to her. He brought her son back to life, gave her joy instead of mourning, restored her hope, and assured her that her crying days were over.

It does not matter what or how much the enemy has stolen from you. Let the giver of life into your space so He can restore all that you've lost (Joel 2:25). Wipe your tears; the master who has the keys of death and Hades has appeared on the scenes, and the enemy must give up his hold. He knows how to restore the past and preserve your future. No matter how acquainted with grief or loss you have become, the Lord is saying to you, "don't cry," because, "I have come to give you life, and to give it more abundantly" (John 10:10). The thief has been caught, and he must restore (Prov. 6:30, 31). You can get your life back as you trust the Lord to compensate you for your loss. It's your season of restoration—wipe your tears, rise up because it's your time to rejoice!

## Personal Reflections/Notes

_____
_____
_____
_____
_____
_____
_____

## Action Steps

_____
_____
_____
_____
_____
_____
_____

# Anna the Prophetess

### Luke 2:36–38

> "She did not depart from the temple, worshiping with fasting and prayer night and day."

Anna, raised by godly parents, lived a good and chaste life as a single woman, and married the man her heart loved. Her life was the picture of perfect bliss until suddenly, seven years into her beautiful marriage her dream turned into a nightmare—her dearly beloved life partner died. There's no record that they had any children in that seven-year period, and it appears like she was left all alone. In her culture and time in history, it was double jeopardy to be widowed so young and to have no offspring. She had every right to be mad at the whole world, to be bitter, like Mara (Naomi), and to question why she was dealt such an ill fate in life, after all her righteous and chaste living.

Anna did not allow herself the luxury of a pity party. Instead, she found a greater purpose for her existence. She became sold out to her King and defender, the Husband of the Widow. She poured out ALL her love on Him, doted on Him, and gave her complete devotion and affection to the Lord alone. She spent countless hours, night and day, in the temple, praying and fasting, watching over God's biggest operation up until that point—the birth of the Messiah and fulfillment of God's promise to mankind from the beginning of creation.

Even though it appeared like she had lost out on good life, societal status, and resources, she turned her loss into great gain by yielding to the Lord in the place of prayer. There she discovered true joy and purpose as she cooperated with God to birth His divine plan of redemption for man. She gained status as God's co-laborer, intercessor, dependable prayer warrior, and faithful soldier who was used of God as she dedicated her life to pray out the will of God for all mankind. Don't allow life's experiences stop you from discovering and going after the higher calling that the Lord has for your life. Yield all your past losses, disappointments, and failures to Him because He alone is able to create beauty out of ashes (Isa. 61:3). He is for YOU!

## Personal Reflections/Notes

_____

_____

_____

_____

_____

_____

_____

## Action Steps

_____

_____

_____

_____

_____

_____

_____

# Eunice

———— ❦ ————

## 2 Timothy 1:5, 3:14, 15; Acts 16: 1–3

Eunice was a woman of faith, with a strong Jewish heritage of faith that she had received from her mother, Lois. She followed the Law faithfully and later on became a follower of Christ. Paul testified of her faith and diligence in teaching her son, Timothy, the scriptures; however, she had married a Greek, a Gentile, a man of a different faith than she had been raised in. It must have been very difficult for her to come around her fellow Jewish believers who had judged her decision to marry a non-Jew as a major *error in judgment*. Eunice, however, remained faithful to the faith she knew and ensured that she passed the same faith along to Timothy despite the prevailing challenges.

She looked beyond her past mistake and nurtured her son to follow Apostle Paul as an ardent disciple, despite his *mixed* background. She raised an evangelist, a man who found a role model and believing father in Paul who gladly and unashamedly introduced Timothy as his son (1 Cor. 4:17; 1 Tim. 1:18, 2 Tim. 2:1). The stigma of not having a Jewish-believing father was removed, and Eunice's commitment to the Lord was chronicled and acknowledged for all to see for all eternity.

No matter what glaring error or mistake you have made in your life, stick with the Lord. He is able to change the trajectory of your life as long as you stay committed to Him and His word. You might have gotten into the wrong relationship or an unequally yoked marriage. Admit your error, and don't lose your faith in the Lord. Don't allow the condemnation from the enemy to keep you away from your Savior and Advocate, Christ Jesus. He is the only hope for your future and your posterity. Let Him step in and raise you and your children as people of uncommon faith, people who will be known, and showcased for the glory of the King.

## Personal Reflections/Notes

_____
_____
_____
_____
_____
_____
_____
_____
_____

## Action Steps

_____
_____
_____
_____
_____
_____
_____
_____
_____

# The Widow and the Unjust Judge

## Luke 18: 1–8

This widow woman had been denied justice for so long that she had begun to lose heart. She had no voice, no advocate or representative, or court-appointed attorney. She was left to fight the system all by herself. She had no choice but to take her case into her own hands and represent herself before a nationally acclaimed corrupt and unjust judge. She was caught within a justice system that allowed such blatant injustice. She knew that on her own, the odds were stacked against her. She had no chance before this judge and his court. She was getting weary of singing the same tune, sounding like a broken record, and getting only radio silence. Somehow, she decided to go in front of this judge one more time.

Then, something unexpected happened. The judge turned around and not only heard her case but awarded her what was rightfully hers. The Righteous Judge had stepped into her case, and instead of the woman getting worn out, she wore the unjust judge out. She outlasted her adversary because she would not quit. She received her victory because she stayed the course, not giving up on the eve of her victory.

I want to encourage you to not quit and go at it one more time. Why? Because you're closer to your victory than you know. Much closer than your circumstances are telling you. Remember that "the darkest hour is just before the dawn," (Thomas Fuller, 1650), and "joy comes in the morning," (Ps. 30:5). Stay the course, hang in just a little longer, give the Righteous Judge some more time. Let your perseverance give God something to work with. Don't drop the case or throw in the towel because your Avenger, the Advocate General of the Church, the Holy Spirit, is working behind the scenes on your behalf, orchestrating your victory, even within an unjust system.

## Personal Reflections/Notes

_____

_____

_____

_____

_____

_____

_____

## Action Steps

_____

_____

_____

_____

_____

_____

_____

# Rahab

— ✺ —

## Joshua 2:1–21, 6:25; Matthew 1:5; James 2:25; Hebrews 11:31

Rahab was in an abhorred and abominable profession—prostitution. It's unknown to us what circumstances led her to choose such a livelihood, but we know her reputation was not one to be desired or emulated. However, she was well known in her trade and was well-positioned with those in authority. In spite of her connections in high places, she was on the path to destruction alongside her fellow Jerichoans. They had no answer for the widely acclaimed prowess and dominance of the God of the Israelites. He defeated all of Israel's enemies in the most unconventional and unprecedented methods of military engagement. She knew that she and her people had no chance against this God. The appearance of the strange men in her neighborhood sealed the deal in her mind.

As soon as she set her eyes on them, she knew that these two men were different. They did not fit the profile of her regular clients. In her usual manner, she took the next step and engaged them in conversation that led to a pact that saved her life and her family. Against her better judgment and instincts, based on her vast experience, she decided to trust these foreign men and put out the scarlet thread as they instructed. She had the hope that the spies will honor their commitment to saving her, and all her relatives who would be with her whenever they returned to destroy the city.

Because she dared to believe in the God of the Jews, her destiny completely changed. She went from a stigmatized prostitute to becoming the great-great-grandmother of King David. Not only that, she got in the lineage of Jesus. Her faith was rewarded not only in the immediate deliverance she experienced when Jericho fell but also in her divine connection to Jesus. Imagine the transformation— God allowed His sinless Son to come through the lineage of a notorious sinner. That is the epitome of God's divine grace and mercy. The enemy may be closing in, but if you stay with God's people and submit to His plan, He will turn the course of your life from disaster to triumph and from defeat to victory. Rahab's story is a clear display of God's abundant grace, His undeserved goodness that turns us from victims to victors, slaves to sons, desecrated to celebrated! In Christ alone!

## Personal Reflections/Notes

_____
_____
_____
_____
_____
_____
_____

## Action Steps

_____
_____
_____
_____
_____
_____

# Ruth

---

## Ruth 3:5–18, 4:9–13, 17; Matthew 1:5

Ruth was young, widowed, childless, and very vulnerable as a foreigner in a strange culture and country, far away from her home country. By herself, she had no chance against the agelong, tradition-steeped cultural practices of the Jewish people who were now her people. In this new environment, she was defenseless and with no status or covering. Her only ally was Naomi, her embittered mother-in-law, who herself was widowed and childless and had lost the desire to fight for anything in life. Ruth had followed Naomi in faith, with a blind loyalty and absolute trust in Naomi's God.

Ruth and Naomi were destitute, poor, and defenseless, with no hope or prospect in the society, until Ruth met Boaz at Naomi's instruction. Boaz redeemed her, restored her dignity, and gave her a coveted status in the same society where she had been despised and downtrodden. Boaz and Ruth went on to have a son named Obed, who became the father of Jesse, the father of David. Many generations later, Jesus came through the lineage of David, referred to as the Son of David. And of His kingdom, there shall be no end (Luke 1:33; Is 9:7).

Life might have dealt you an unfair blow, and you feel the urge to live with a chip on your shoulder because you've had it rougher than anyone else you know. Refuse to give in to bitterness because bitterness opens the door for the enemy to steal more from you. Ruth overcame loss and disappointment by turning to the God of Naomi even when Naomi herself was upset at God. Ruth was able to rise above her pain by God's divine grace, as she refused to become bitter toward God and people.

If you will accept Jesus's move to enter into your situation and turn things around, then your latter end can be gloriously better than your beginning, and you too can become a history maker. Don't let your history define you and your future. Partner with the God who has the ability to redefine history through your life. Ruth refused to be history; she rose up and made history. You're next if you'll do what Ruth did—refuse to get stuck, trust God, and get back up again!

## Personal Reflections/Notes

_____

_____

_____

_____

_____

_____

_____

## Action Steps

_____

_____

_____

_____

_____

_____

# The Syrophoenician Woman

## Mathew 15: 21–25; Mark 7:25–30

This mother knew without a doubt that her daughter's condition was far from ordinary. It was obvious to her that her daughter was severely tormented by an evil spirit, but she felt powerless against such an evil force. On her own, she could not help her precious little girl. Her helplessness was compounded by her status as a foreigner among the Jews and, therefore, had no access to Jesus. She had heard that He had power against evil spirits and could help her daughter. Her resolve to get her daughter the much-needed help led her to Jesus, as she defied all obstacles and oppositions, even from Jesus and His disciples.

She heard firsthand from Jesus that her daughter did not qualify for the help she was seeking. Healing was the *children's bread*, and her daughter did not have the same status as *the childre*n. She was told that her daughter was ineligible because she was not of the *lost house of Israel*. Even worse, she was referred to as a dog—if the ineligibility was not bad enough, the name-calling would have done it. She would have been gravely offended, justifiably so, and stomped off in a huff. However, rather than take offense, she saw an opportunity. The deliverer was at least willing to talk to her, hear her plea, and not send her off without giving her an audience. That was all the opening she needed because desperate things require desperate measures. She was going to hang on to every word of the master, who was the only option for her daughter's freedom from demonic oppression.

She refused to let offense keep her daughter bound. She had to break through. Instead of pain, she allowed faith to rise within her. Healing was available but, in this case, only for a select group. She went for the crumbs—that was all she could get her hands on, but that will be enough for her daughter's deliverance. She was aware that she could not alter her daughter's natural heritage, but she was going to seek an exception to the rule if possible. She made a bold and unusual request, grabbed onto grace, and received what she was naturally ineligible for. All she had was a mustard seed faith, but that was more than enough! The mustard seed faith gets the job done every time! She held onto the smallest flicker of light, the tiny crack in the door, and got into the place where her faith drew out her miracle. The result was that *her daughter was healed instantly*.

Are you determined to work with the smallest ounce of faith you have? Will you work with the little you have? That is all that the Lord is asking for. Has the enemy lied to you about how ineligible you are for whatever reason? Maybe you don't have a "big faith," or you don't have the title or qualification needed for your desired miracle or promotion? It's a lie—that's all it is—a boldface lie. Right now, the Master is waiting for your move; for you to take a small step forward with the mustard seed faith that you have. Will you do it? Your total deliverance and miracle are waiting on the other end of your step of faith. Go forward and go for it in Jesus's name!

## Personal Reflections/Notes

_____
_____
_____
_____
_____
_____
_____

## Action Steps

_____

_____

_____

_____

_____

_____

_____

# Martha

— ∽ —

## Luke 10:38–42; John 11

Martha was an excellent hostess, an extremely hospitable woman with a warm personality. She was always eager to open her home to host friends and family. Martha was a great *doer*, always on the go, actively moving and creating things, great at multitasking. She was doing her best to ensure that Jesus and his entourage were comfortable and well taken care of when they came visiting her home in Bethany. She was playing the role of the perfect hostess, making sure everything was flawless—the food, place setting, decorations, the whole nine yards.

She was rather befuddled and thoroughly embarrassed by her sister Mary's unacceptable attitude. Mary knew they were expecting guests, and the moment Jesus came in, she abandoned everything and went and sat with the men and other guests, leaving Martha to finish up all the preparation and setting up. How insensitive. What a slap on the good training their mother had given them. She tried to get Mary's attention, but she was too engrossed in what Jesus was saying. What could be more important than getting food ready for Jesus after he would have been preaching for so long? When she could no longer take it, she interrupted Jesus mid-sentence and rebuked both Him and Mary for such insensitivity. She was left to do all the work by herself, and Jesus condoned such thoughtlessness from Mary. She instructed Him to send Mary to the kitchen where she rightfully belonged.

Martha was assured in her own mind that she was right, and they were wrong. In her self-righteous state, she knew she was justified in her decision to serve rather than listen to Jesus teach. Also, she was justified in calling both Jesus and Mary out on this atrocious conduct. When Jesus kindly but firmly said to her, "Martha, Martha, you are worried and troubled about many things; but ONE thing is needful…and Mary has chosen it," she realized that she had judged the situation wrong and misplaced her priority altogether.

Oftentimes, we pride ourselves in our activities and service opportunities, done in the Lord's name and for His people. However, we neglect His need to just be with us, asking for our undivided attention, in a quiet, calm, undisturbed moment, just to fellowship with Him. To hear His voice, be fully immersed in Him, with nothing being more important to us than to be with the lover of our souls, and to learn at His feet. He's asking you and I to forget for a moment the needs that we and others have, and to be reminded that He who fed thousands with so little is able to take care of your next meal. In this moment, put everything aside and just focus on being with Jesus, listening for His voice and heart. Make seeking Him the most important thing to you right now, your number one priority, no matter what else is calling for your attention.

Action: Pause for the next five minutes and just listen for the Lord. Put every distraction away and just focus on Him. Write down your experience below. Make this a regular practice as you develop a deeper relationship with the Lord.

## Personal Reflections

_____

_____

_____

_____

_____

_____

_____

_____

_____

_____

# Abigail

_____ ∽ _____

## 1 Samuel 25:2–42, 2 Samuel 3:3; 1 Chronicle 3:1

### From Wife of a Fool to Wife of a King

Abigail was a beautiful, witty, intelligent, discerning, highly resource-ful, gifted communicator and mediator, a woman full of wisdom. Unfortunately, she unequally yoked in marriage to a prideful fool, Nabal. Her husband was the very opposite of everything good in Abigail—he was mean, harsh, evil, brutish, and a very poor commu-nicator. Somehow, he was very wealthy and had a lot of resources. Strangely, Abigail was a dutiful wife who stayed loyal to Nabal, managing his home and business, ensuring he continued to prosper financially. How did she end up with such a man?

Your guess is as good as mine. We could presume a few rea-sons—maybe it was a forced or arranged marriage, maybe, he enticed her with his riches, or maybe Nabal changed after marriage. The Bible does not give us insight into why and how she got married to Nabal. We still are left wondering how she got under the leadership of a man who had no regard for anyone but himself.

Her connection to Nabal put her at risk of losing everything she had ever worked for all in one day, about to perish with her husband because of his rash decision and provoking speech against David, the anointed King. When Abigail was informed of the impending doom, she decided to finally take her life and her entire household into her hands and save everyone from annihilation using her wisdom. She not only brought abundant supplies to David and his men; she spoke with him in honor, speaking into his future and God-ordained purpose. She helped him avert a major error in his life—reactional massacre based on irrational anger. He would have acted like a fool also, in response to a fool.

In her wisdom, Abigail brought salvation to two large groups—Nabal's and David's. Her accurate assessment and report on her husband as she spoke to David saved the day. Using her insight, she waited for the right time to confront Nabal of his foolishness, and his heart could not take it. His death, not at the hand of any man, became her freedom. She went from wife (and now widow) of a fool to the wife of a king. What a transformation!

Are you caught in an impossible relationship, a covenant that is threatening your identity and purpose in life? Turn to the Lord and trust Him to give you a way out, not a man-made deliverance. God does not change the blueprint that He put together for anyone of us, no matter how many detours we take. Believe God for a customized, heaven-designed escape into the fullest life your Father has created for you. Let hope for a better tomorrow arise within you today!

## Personal Reflections

_____

_____

_____

_____

_____

_____

## Action Steps

_____

_____

_____

_____

_____

_____

# Lydia

—— ⌘ ——

## Acts 16:11–15

Lydia was a very successful businesswoman who had found the God of the Jews. She had already converted from her Gentile ways to Judaism and was meeting regularly with other women to pray. From all appearances, she was doing well until she met the Apostle Paul, who introduced her to the Lord Jesus Christ. Her heart was opened by the Lord to receive all that Paul talked about as he shared the good news. Lydia was one hungry woman! She took it all in and went from mere religion to a very personal relationship with God. Not only her, but also her entire household followed her example and got baptized, making a public declaration of their commitment to follow Jesus and live for Him.

If you stay hungry for more of God, He is faithful to satisfy you and fill you up with His goodness and His word. He will send you the word you need to move higher and higher in your understanding of Him and His ways. How do you work up a hunger for the God who alone can satisfy? By developing a strong desire for His Word and His presence through daily prayer, praise, thanksgiving, worship, and time in His Word (Ps. 42:1, 2).

Lydia acted immediately on her newfound faith and status as a member of the household of God. She made her home available to the servants of God who had ministered to her. She not only received the message; she also received the messengers. "Believe the Lord your God (His word) and you will be established, believe (receive) His servants and you will prosper," (1 Chron. 20:20).

Like Lydia, be quick to bless others with the resources that God has put into your hands. "Do good to all men, and especially to those of the household of faith," (Gal. 6:10). As you develop in your personal relationship with the Lord, seek to develop in your relationship with His people, your fellow brothers, and sisters in the Lord. As you go through your day today, ask yourself, *Who can I minister to today?*

## Personal Reflections/Notes

_____
_____
_____
_____
_____
_____
_____

## Action Steps

_____
_____
_____
_____
_____
_____
_____

# Dorcas

---

## Acts 9:36–42

Dorcas was a woman with a large heart. She had dedicated her life to doing good works for God's people. She was a selfless giver who was committed to serving with joy, working with her hands to serve others in the name of the Lord. She had become well known for her good deeds and *goodies*. Dorcas made hand-crafted clothes sewn together with stitches of love. She created exquisite and unique pieces for all who came by. Dorcas was everybody's *mama*, *nana*, and sister.

Then, Dorcas fell sick, in spite of all her good acts. Nobody could make sense of how a bad thing could happen to such a good person. People must have come together to pray for Dorcas, expecting her to recover, but instead, she died. What a sad day—everyone was thrown into mourning, crying, despair, with lots of questions. Who could replace Dorcas in their lives?

Suddenly, someone remembered (stirred by the Holy Spirit) that Apostle Peter was close by in Lydda, and they quickly sent for him. Thankfully, he responded to their call and came to Dorcas' home in Joppa. Some of these people were there when Jesus raised Lazarus from the dead, but they had not seen anybody else perform such a miracle. They were still wailing and telling Peter all about Dorcas and how good she had been to them all. Peter did what he had seen his Master do—he put the mourners and criers out and faced death without fear.

By the power of the Holy Spirit, Peter called Dorcas's departed spirit back to life, and she broke out of the grip of death and sat up in bed! Dorcas received another lease of life, another opportunity to do even greater works! Whatever has died in your life, be it a dream, desire, or vision, expect a rising up today. A resurrection back to life, a new beginning, catch the wind in your sails, because the Master is here! He never gives up on any of us as long as we don't give up. He has the power and willingness to bring the dead back to life right now! He's not done with you yet! Receive new life today! Write down one thing that you are trusting the Lord to resurrect in your life today. Surrender it in the place of prayer and watch Him do the impossible.

## Personal Reflections/Notes

_____

_____

_____

_____

_____

_____

_____

_____

_____

_____

## Action Steps

_____

_____

_____

_____

_____

_____

_____

_____

_____

_____

# The Widow of Zarephath

———— ∽ ————

## 1 Kings 17:8–24

This woman had lost her husband and was left to raise their son alone, in the midst of famine. We're not sure how or what led to her husband's demise—starvation from the famine, another disease, accident? Maybe he had selflessly and slowly starved himself to death in an effort to preserve his wife and son, and now, she has found herself on a similar path. It was the end of the road for her and her son, and she saw no way out. She was planning their last meal when she *ran into* the man of God who asked for the impossible—her one and final meal.

She had no problems getting him water, but then he dared to ask for more! A cake! She did not spare him an earful of her woes and hopeless situation. She was convinced that after her spill, he would withdraw his request and be on his merry way. He instead persisted and gave her a sure word from the Lord that not only preserved her life but resulted in the saving of her son's life—twice! The first *salvation* was from death from famine, and the second one was from sudden death from an unknown cause. This woman's obedience to the word of the Lord, in the mouth of His servant, changed the trajectory of her life and her story forever! Talk about an alternate ending to a movie or story.

This unnamed woman's obedience and hospitality brought tremendous gain into her life. She stepped out in faith, out of hopelessness into fresh hope, out of sure defeat into perpetual victory, out of obscurity into a celebrity—her story has given her eternal prominence. Her obedience paved the way for her miracle. What was the last instruction you received from the Lord? What have you done with it? Your promotion is at the end of your obedience. Don't delay any further, receive grace to obey, and see your life begin to transform and take on a fresh start.

## Personal Reflections/Notes

_____

_____

_____

_____

_____

_____

_____

## Action Steps

_____

_____

_____

_____

_____

_____

_____

# Hannah

⁂

## 1 Samuel 1:1–28, 1 Samuel 2: 1–11, 18–21

Hannah was despised, disdained, ridiculed, and mercilessly mocked at by Peninah. Why? Because Hannah had an obvious lack and deficiency—barrenness. She had no children and was considered a burden on the system—nonproductive, lacking output, with nothing to show for being a wife to Elkanah. In spite of her husband's sweet affirmation of her worth to him, Hannah could not give up the deep and burning desire to be productive; to birth her own children, and show proof of her womanhood. Peninah, her rival, was the epitome of fertility—she seemed to effortlessly produce babies, and she was eager to let Hannah see how happy she was to have those children running around the house. She taunted Hannah with intense cruelty and tore at the core of her being. Hannah plunged into depression despite the unwavering love and devotion of her husband. Her shame and pain were daily with her.

Suddenly, Hannah got desperate enough to step out in faith, all by herself. She decided to go and fight alone for her destiny before the Lord, whom she trusted, to reverse her situation. She stopped looking to her husband or anybody else for her happiness. She took back the control she had outsourced to Mrs. Peninah and her husband and took the matter to the God of Israel. Her story would not have changed unless she had taken the bold step, on her own, away from her usual annual practice. In her one-on-one session with the Lord, she poured out her heart to Him—her pain, missed opportunities, unfulfilled expectations, everything. She asked the Giver of Life for a son that she was going to give back to the Lord.

Hannah made her need secondary to the Lord's need of a man—a prophet who would speak on His behalf and do His will in Israel. Her story changed when she made the connection and decided to wrap her most desired need in God's purpose and will. She not only got Samuel; she received five other children from the Lord. In addition to turning her fortune around, God used her life to reveal His eternal purpose for mankind forever. God not only gave her a great return for her seed but also inspired her to speak prophetically about Jesus's coming to the world as our Savior. Hannah gave her ONLY begotten son, Samuel, her most priced treasure, totally to the Lord.

What need do you have that is so paramount on your heart? Why not give it to the Lord as a seed and trust Him to turn it into a huge harvest that will outlast you and speak for generations to come, and for eternity?

## Personal Reflections/Notes

_____
_____
_____
_____
_____
_____
_____

## Action Steps

_____
_____
_____
_____
_____
_____
_____

# The Widow with a Vessel of Oil

## 2 Kings 4:1–7

The enemy had done a number on her family. Her husband, a devout, God-fearing servant of God, had died, leaving his family in deep debt. It was already hard before he died, now it's beyond hard. After burying him, this woman had to deal with the mountain of financial debt that confronted her and her sons. The creditor had determined his payment: her two sons. They will both be taken into slavery until they can pay back every dime owed. She knew she had no voice or advocate against her creditor. She was on the verge of being stripped of every valuable thing in her life.

Suddenly, she remembered that there was a prophet in the land. She reached out to him for help, and he asked her a strange question, "what do you have?" She had just told him how much in the deficit they were, and he thought she had something. If she did, she would not be here. She did not think she had anything—her creditor and credit rating proved that. She was under the barrel, and nothing she had could make a difference. At that moment, she remembered that she did have something. She blurted out, "I have a little vessel of oil in my house." That was enough for the man of God to work with for her miracle to happen.

The man of God gave her specific instructions which she followed diligently and broke out of debt and into abundant living—she and her two sons. God not only turned her life around; he restored her wealth. Right before her eyes, her little vessel became a reservoir that filled multiple oil vessels. Instead of running dry, she experienced an overflow. In place of her lack, she received lavish provision. She went from abject lack to a place of abundance.

What do you have in your hands? In your house, in your life? Are you letting someone or a financial institution determine your worth? Whose report or account are you living by? The creditor or God's report? No matter how hopeless your situation is, never forget that you always have something. You have your praise, your breath, your life—that means you have hope. Hope in a God that can save, deliver, and turn things around for your good and for His glory. Acknowledge what He has given you and let praise rise within you so the eyes of your understanding can be opened to clearly see the path of escape and prosperity that He has prepared for you. Write down your answer to the question: *What do you have?*

## Personal Reflections/Notes

_____

_____

_____

_____

_____

_____

_____

_____

## Action Steps

_____

_____

_____

_____

_____

_____

_____

_____

# Bathsheba

───────── ✑ ─────────

## 2 Samuel 11:2–27; 12:24–25;
## 1 Kings 1:11–34; Mathew 1:6

Bathsheba was living a stable, undisturbed life, an offspring of God-fearing parents, married to the man of her dreams, valiant Uriah. Uriah was a man of integrity and extreme loyalty to the King and the nation of Israel. Bathsheba enjoyed life in her community, living simply and without any problems until a man in authority violated her and took advantage of her in the cruelest way. King David, a man that she and her husband held in highest honor as God's representative, had forced her to break her vow to her husband by lying with him. She was powerless against the king and the system that allowed him to get away with such excesses and abuse of his office. As she was trying to put the confusion and humiliation behind her, she discovered that she was pregnant. How could a one-time encounter produce such life-altering and everlasting impact?

While she was still trying to make sense of all that happened and wondering how to tell Uriah about her ordeal, he returned home from his current deployment unannounced. Unbeknown to her, she became part of a scheme to make her husband lie with her and foist the pregnancy on him. However, Uriah's integrity and sense of responsibility would not allow him to have any sexual contact with her. Before she knew it, he was redeployed to the war, never to return home. She never had the chance to tell him her story. Her loyal, heroic husband paid the ultimate sacrifice, laid down his life for the country he loved, paid the price to protect the woman he adored, and the king he deeply honored. Did Uriah die on her account? Bathsheba would never know what he knew and would never be able to tell Uriah how much she still loved him. Her heart was completely shattered and heavily burdened.

Now, she was widowed from the man she loved, pregnant for a man that she did not choose, or love. Soon she moved to the palace. Living in luxury but miserable. She missed her simple life that had now turned upside down in a flash. She had the hope that she would at least be comforted at the birth of her baby. But alas, the son she labored over died because of the Lord's wrath. What else could go wrong in her life? She was at the end of her rope—no Uriah, no baby, now trapped in a loveless relationship. Deep in despair, despondent, a classic victim of circumstances, she watched her carefully planned life crumble before her, like a pack of cards.

However, our merciful, loving God comforted her by giving her another son—Jedidiah, which means "one that the Lord loves." She bore a son that will change the world. The Lord revealed Himself to her as the restorer. Her story was not yet over. God was about to turn all her calamities around and give her a brand-new beginning. Not only did she become David's queen and confidant; she became his beloved. Her broken heart was able to heal and love again. She was given the grace to nurture and raise the wisest human being in history and was named in the Savior's lineage. She did not allow her past to permanently damage and paralyze her. She did not allow her past to overtake her future. She let the Lord heal, empower, and elevate her to a place of influence and leadership that she was born to occupy.

Don't let tragedy lock you into a life of misery and insignificance. Let love lift you up. Let supernatural forgiveness elevate you above your circumstances. Allow God's grace to turn you from a victim to a victor, through Christ Jesus!

# Sarah

———— ✌ ————

Genesis 12:1–5, 10–20, 16:1–6, 17:5–15,
16–19, 21, 18:6–10, 11–15, 20:1–18, 21:1–7,
8–13, 23:1,19; 1 Peter 3:8; Hebrew 11:11


She judged Him faithful who had promised.
—Heb. 11:11 NKJV

She considered Him who had given her the promise
to be reliable and true [to His word].
—Heb. 11:11 AMP

This testimony in Hebrews 11 about Sarah's faith is very encouraging. Sarai had been barren all her life; from her teens through twenties and thirties, middle age, later age, peri- and post-menopausal period, until all hope of ever having a biological child by any means known was gone. Even the best and most advanced gynecologists and scientists of her time had stopped trying.

Yet, Abraham still called her *princess* because God had instructed him to change her name at eighty-nine years of age. He was ninety-nine years old when she started calling him, "Abraham, Father of many nations," purely because God had instructed them to do so. They both changed their names based on God's word, not on their natural circumstances or feelings. Even though nothing around them pointed to the remotest possibility of a baby coming out of their very old bodies, they acted on the word that God had given them (Gen. 17:5, 16, 19, 21). Because of her faith and decision to hold

God's word as dependable and trustworthy, she not only conceived, she carried her pregnancy to term. Sarah delivered a miracle baby, Laughter, whom she had the pleasure of raising to a full-grown man of thirty-seven years at the time of her death.

Sarah had written herself off—long before the Angel appeared and told her the most ludicrous thing she had ever heard—baby at ninety years. It was indeed laughable. No wonder she laughed to herself. But the humorous God that we serve not only brought His good word to pass, He named the child Isaac (meaning laughter)! The same God (Heb. 13:8) who brought laughter to Sarah is able to make you laugh over the situation you're currently experiencing. No matter how impossible in the natural your situation is, a word from the Lord will turn things around for you. Your faith and firm decision to stay with God's word will produce the miracle, bringing you intense joy and laughter all your days!

What are you chuckling over right now? What is that impossible situation that makes you want to laugh because it's so ridiculous, it's not even funny? Trust the Lord for His divine intervention and He will make you laugh out loud, at last.

## Personal Reflections/Notes

_____

_____

_____

_____

_____

_____

## Action Steps

_____

_____

_____

_____

_____

_____

# Elizabeth

—— ❦ ——

## Luke 1:5–7, 23–25, 39–45, 57–66, 67–80

Elizabeth had a pedigree—from the lineage of old priests, a daughter of Aaron, and married to a priest. She stayed within the lines, and therefore, was expected to flourish and live a fruitful life as a wife and mother. However, despite her heritage and righteous living, Elizabeth was barren, without a child to call her own. Elizabeth, a woman of God, the wife of a man of God, full of righteousness and devoted to the Lord, yet she had to bear the reproach of barrenness for several years. She and Zechariah had given up any hope of having children when Angel Gabriel showed up and announced to Zechariah that he and Elizabeth were going to have a son named John. John will be the forerunner of the Messiah. Zechariah was in shock and his little brain could not comprehend the message he had just received.

Elizabeth received the word and conceived in her advanced years. In spite of her obvious need, Elizabeth never quit serving God and entrusting her life to Him. Nothing took her attention off the Lord. Nothing compared to a deep, committed, intimate relationship with her God, Jehovah El Shaddai. Elizabeth's lack did not hinder or take away her service. She kept her focus right where it belonged—on the Lord, and not on her lack or need.

Elizabeth's prayers that she thought had been forgotten or unheard; were actually heard. Just like God was mindful of Elizabeth's prayers, be encouraged that God is mindful of your prayers. He NEVER forgets. Don't let the passage of time discourage you and make you give up on the desired end result that God promised you. Stay faithful; your answer is closer than you think. Like Elizabeth, keep your eyes fixed on Jesus, the starter and completer of your faith (Heb. 12:2).

## Personal Reflections/Notes

_____
_____
_____
_____
_____
_____
_____
_____
_____
_____

## Action Steps

_____
_____
_____
_____
_____
_____
_____
_____
_____
_____

# Rebecca

~

## Genesis 24:12–67

Rebecca was an answer to prayer—an instant answer. Abraham's head servant, Eliezer, had prayed and asked a specific request of the Lord as he went on his mission to get Isaac a wife from Abraham's people. Just as Eliezer concluded his prayer, Rebecca showed up and fulfilled everything he had prayed for, to the tee.

Her spirited and encouraging attitude toward a total stranger was unprecedented. She was an eager helper. She not only gave him a drink but also volunteered to get water for his animals. Talk about a servant's heart. God had been preparing her through the numerous service opportunities that she had had—at home, on the job, in the community, and so on. She probably was unaware that her everyday attitude toward serving others was going to bring her into her divine destiny. She literally walked into the deal without any foreknowledge of Eliezer's prayer or mission in her hometown.

Her excellent attitude brought her into favor and got her immediate rewards and tangible gifts. But more importantly, into the lineage of Jesus, the Christ, the Messiah, the Anointed One. She became a matriarch, mother of Esau and Jacob, the Jacob who became Israel, Prince with God, Father of the people of covenant that God predetermined long before she was born.

Like the Bible says in Galatians 6:9 (MSG), "So let's not allow ourselves to get fatigued doing good. At the right time we will harvest a good crop if we don't give up, or quit." Serve with every opportunity you have as unto the Lord. Give Him your best every time. Train yourself to serve the best you know with every opportunity.

Your next act of service might be just what will open the door to your next adventure and into the amazing future that God has prepared for you!

Question to Ponder: What steps can I take to make my service five-star level every time?

Scriptures to review: Col. 3:17, 23, 24 (TPT, NLT, ERV); Eccl. 9:10 (NLT, MSG); 1 Cor. 10:31 (AMPC, TPT).

## Personal Reflections/Notes

_____

_____

_____

_____

_____

_____

_____

## Action Steps

_____

_____

_____

_____

_____

_____

_____

# Rachel

## Genesis 29:9–30, 30:1–2, 22–24

Beautiful Rachel, well-loved, desired, and sought after. She was Jacob's beloved. Jacob happily labored for seven years to have Rachel as his wife, but he was tricked into marrying Leah, her older sister. He then served another seven years to be able to have Rachel as his wife forever. Many years after Rachel had married Jacob, her sweetheart and first love, she found herself with a huge and unfulfilled desire. She desperately wanted a baby of her own, especially because Leah had given Jacob many sons. In her desperation, she threatened Jacob with suicide if he didn't give her a child. She had misplaced and misdirected her anger, driven by envy and disdain for her rival, her sister, and Jacob, her husband, who continued to love her dearly and unconditionally.

Rachel had forgotten that natural human love is very inferior to God's love and capability. In due time God gave Rachel an extraordinary son, Joseph, who would become the deliverer of the people of God. No matter how loving and dedicated your spouse, father, mother, sister, brother, or children, they are severely limited in what they can do or get for you. Don't mistake them for your source because they are not, and they are incapable of taking on that role. Keep your eyes on the one and only source of every good thing you could ever desire. Develop your personal faith in God, the unfailing, unchanging source of every good thing. He never runs dry and never runs out. God will get you what you need and desire, according to His riches in glory by Christ Jesus.

## Questions to Ponder

1. In what area(s) of your life have you set up someone or something (e.g. your job) as your source?
2. What steps can you take to make God your ONLY source for every area of your life?

## Personal Reflections/Notes

_____
_____
_____
_____
_____
_____
_____

## Action Steps

_____
_____
_____
_____
_____
_____
_____

# Jochebed

───── ❧ ─────

## Exodus 2:1–10; 6:20, 26–27; Numbers 26:59; Hebrews 11:23

Jochebed was a woman of exemplary faith and courage. She knew she could trust God to save Moses, her precious son, from sure death as the Pharaoh had decreed. Jochebed, fearless and discerning, defied the Pharaoh's evil order to kill all male babies born to the children of Israel. Instead, she relied on God for divine ideas on how to preserve Moses from his birth to the time he was rescued by the enemy's daughter. Her act of uncommon faith led not only to Moses's salvation but to the deliverance of the entire nation of Israel from centuries of bondage and brutal slavery.

In Jochebed's time, there was no 3D ultrasound to reveal the gender of her baby so she could plan ahead. As Jochebed anticipated and prepared for the birth of her baby, she could not deny the fact that he might be born to die. If she had a female baby, all was well. If he was a male, he already had a death sentence hanging over his head before he had a chance to live.

In due time, Jochebed had her baby, and behold, it was a special son! She knew by law, he was to die, but she chose to follow God's plan and decree and fought for his right to live. She discerned that he was no ordinary child and decided that he was going to live even if it cost her own life. She carefully hid him for three months, against all odds, risking her entire family's life to save Moses's. Her fearlessness and dependence on God led her to build an ark for Moses, to preserve him from evil, ferry him to safety, and begin his extraordinary journey to greatness. She sought God's plan and direction every step of the carefully planned project. She positioned Miriam to watch over the ark as it sailed on the crocodile-infested Nile River.

God honored her faith and boldness by working out outstanding miracles that resulted in her getting paid to raise her son Moses. The river that was meant to drown him elevated him, and the King that was set to destroy him raised and nurtured him as a grandson. What an awesome God we serve!

Jochebed, an outstanding woman of faith, ended up raising three exceptional children—Miriam, Aaron, and Moses because she saw beyond the ordinary and anchored her faith in the God who is able to do extraordinary things. Like Jochebed, if you put your focus on God and His word, and refuse to be overwhelmed by the evil in the world around you and your children, you will ride on those very things that were meant to destroy you and your posterity. You will be able to say with blessed assurance, "I will not fear, what can man do to me" (Ps. 118: 6)? What unrighteous decree or law is looming over you? Take your attention off it and reset your focus on the Lord. Then, watch him turn all in your favor!

## Personal Reflections/Notes

_____

_____

_____

_____

_____

## Action Steps

_____

_____

_____

_____

_____

# Puah and Shiphrah

⸝∽⸍

## Exodus 1:15–20

Puah and her professional colleague Shiphrah were two courageous Hebrew midwives who defied the word of the world leader of their time. Because the words of the king ran crosswise to the word of God, they chose to obey God rather than the king. These women were skilled and well known in their chosen field throughout the nation. The Pharaoh instructed them to kill every male child born to any Hebrew woman. He recruited them to carry out his mission of infanticide in his bid to curtail the growth of the Hebrew nation.

Their obedience to the king had potential benefits, including his approval and endorsement, and possible expansion of their business. They also were at major risk of losing their business, reputation, and possibly, their lives if they chose to disobey the king. However, they sided with God, disobeyed the king's evil law, and preserved the Hebrew boys alive. When the king summoned them, they were bold to declare to him that, "the Hebrew women are not like the Egyptian women." Since they would not carry out the king's orders, he made it everybody else's responsibility to get rid of their neighbor's male babies.

Puah and Shiphrah's obedience and boldness in the face of adversity led to the preservation of many sons in Israel, including Moses, Israel's deliverer from centuries of slavery. In their obedience, they submitted themselves totally to the will of the Lord and His instructions to save lives rather than destroy innocent lives. In due time, God rewarded them by preserving them, their work, reputation, and they received families of their own. As they took care of God's family, God took care of their families.

In what areas are you compromising and yielding to fear? Are you choosing God's word over your natural senses and reasoning? Determine to stay with whatever instruction the Lord has given to you. Elevate His word above the word of any human being or system. Refuse to yield to the temptation to succumb to unrighteous decrees out of fear. God will always come through for anyone who chooses His word over the word of any man or man-made system. He will reward your labor of love as you minister to His people and do your best to fulfill His divine purpose for your life and community. Refuse to take the easy road but rather stay on the high road that always leads to victory, honor, and promotion!

## Personal Reflections/Notes

_____
_____
_____
_____
_____
_____
_____

## Action Steps

_____
_____
_____
_____
_____
_____
_____

# The Poor Widow with Two Mites

*⚬*

## Mark 12:41–44; Luke 21:1–4

> She gave God all that she had to live on,
> which was everything she had.
> —Mark 12:41 TPT

> All the others gave what they'll never miss,
> she gave extravagantly what she
> couldn't afford—she gave her all.
>
> —MSG

Often times, self-preservation gets the better of all of us. It pushes us to want to hold on to what we have and reserve the little resource that is barely enough to sustain us. This pitifully poor widow with no support system or safety net came into the temple; and rather than hold back the measly two mites she had, she decided to give it all. After her giving, she had nothing left. That was all that she had left to her name, and she gave it all! Rather than do the most rational thing of saving the little she had, she chose to release it all to the Lord. Not allowing herself to worry about where her next supply will come from, she decided to trust the Lord, Jehovah Jireh, the Provider, completely, with reckless abandon.

Guess who noticed her giving? Jesus, the Master, and Most Righteous Judge. Jesus judged her action as righteous. He didn't notice her giving because of the amount—that was not what caught the Lord's attention. Her heart and implicit trust in the Lord impressed Jesus. That caught His attention. Next time somebody asks for your *widow's mite,* remember that it's not the smallest bill in your wallet that the widow's mite represents—it's your best, your all, your everything!

If you're down to your last supply, what will you do with it? Spend it, save it, or release it? Spending it means the end of all your supply—everything used up. Saving it produces a small hope of an increase in the future, which is not guaranteed. It also means you don't have it to use in your moment of lack. Releasing it into the hands of the all-sufficient God guarantees that not only will He notice your giving, but He will also reward your obedience and selfless heart.

Determine today to give Him not only your best but your all! Ask God for His grace to trust and obey Him and know that His everlasting arms will not fail you. He has promised to take care of you as you daily cast all your cares on Him.

## Personal Reflections/Notes

_____

_____

_____

_____

_____

_____

_____

_____

## Action Steps

_____

_____

_____

_____

_____

_____

_____

_____

# Deborah

—— ∽ ——

## Judges 4, 5

As a Mother in Israel, Deborah rose to the occasion and led the people of God out of oppression and fear. She was a brave and decisive national leader who helped Barak gain the victory after she gave him the word from the Lord. She told General Barak that God had promised victory in the upcoming battle. But Barak would not go to the battle alone. He invited Deborah to accompany him to the battle because that affirmed her conviction about the word she gave. Going with her meant he would not receive the full credit for the triumph in battle.

Deborah will share the glory with him. Barak was fine with that outcome. Deborah was very aware of her role and her gender as a female leader. She was unapologetically female, letting Barak know in her *acceptance speech* to him that she was going to take her share of the credit for the conquest. It was not a popular thing to do in her day and time. She did not downplay who she was—a woman, a prophetess, a wife to Lapidot, and a national leader.

Deborah wore her multiple hats well. In all her roles, she represented the Lord skillfully, using every influence to advance God's purpose in her nation. Her assertiveness and bravery made her stand out among others. In the midst of her accomplishments, she maintained her identity as a spokesperson for God.

What role(s) has the Lord called you to fulfill? What assignment(s) have you been given by your Creator? He has packaged within you every attribute and resource that you need to succeed in your God-given assignment. Get comfortable with being you.

Celebrate who the Lord has made you. And like Deborah, rise to the occasion and let your light shine for others to see so they may give glory to your Father in heaven.

## Personal Reflections/Notes

_____

_____

_____

_____

_____

_____

_____

## Action Steps

_____

_____

_____

_____

_____

_____

_____

# The Shunamite Woman

## 2 Kings 4: 8–37

"All is well," is all she said when she was asked about her dead son's state. She called those things that be not as though they were, rather than speak those things as they were. Who is this woman of faith? All we know is that she is a woman from Shunem. A notable woman for many reasons. She was well known in her society as a faithful wife, a wise, hospitable, and compassionate woman. Most importantly, she was known as a woman of uncommon faith who chose to speak her desired outcome over her son rather than merely state the fact of his death.

As a woman of remarkable means, she generously (and without strings attached) gave her resources to minister to Elisha, a man of God who frequently passed through her town. She convinced her husband to build a penthouse for the comfort of Elisha and his servant, Gehazi, as they journeyed through Shunem on their ministerial assignments. She displayed great integrity in giving to the man of God without expecting anything in return. She never made a demand on him nor call for favors because of her generosity toward him. Yet, she had a huge need in her life. She gave her resources unconditionally. She was not trading her resources for the prophet's anointing or spiritual gifts. Her generous and sincere giving and ministry to Prophet Elisha opened up his heart to declare God's blessing, unsolicited, into her life, in her area of greatest need.

How are you giving? Are you truly giving, or are you trading? Do you give with strings attached? Expecting to receive a return from the person/people you give to or from Jehovah, the Lord of the harvest? Are you expecting to reap from whom you have sown to, or are you looking to the Lord and expecting your reward from Him alone? Make up your mind to be more deliberate in your giving—of your time, service, skills, money; with all your heart, in sincerity, and truth. Ask the Lord to help you to give, every time, with your eyes on Him.

## Personal Reflections/Notes

_____
_____
_____
_____
_____
_____
_____

## Action Steps

_____
_____
_____
_____
_____
_____
_____

# Priscilla

## Acts 18:2, 24–28; Romans 16:3; 1 Corinthians 16:19; 2 Timothy 4:19

"My helpers in Christ Jesus"—that's the description that Apostle Paul gave to Priscilla and her husband, Aquila. Together, they faithfully served with every opportunity and gift that they had. Priscilla ministered alongside Paul. She supported his work, traveled with his evangelistic team, started and nurtured a home church, and mentored Apollos. Priscilla and Aquila had found in Apollos an uncommon zeal and eagerness to proclaim God's word, but he needed some depth in the word.

So Priscilla welcomed young Apollos into her home and heart and created an opportunity for intense and personal discipleship. She went on to minister to him and prepared him for the ministry that God had called him into. Apollos became an outstanding gospel minister, placed in the same category as the Apostle Paul. The success of his ministry can be traced back to the diligence of Priscilla and Aquila, who poured into him tirelessly till he had developed the spiritual maturity he needed to teach God's word with boldness.

Who has God called you to mentor and nurture and groom in the faith? Do your best to pour into them. Take your work seriously, be diligent with the one person that God has sent your way. You never know what impact the Lord has determined for your mentee to make on this side of eternity. If you are yet to identify your mentee, ask the Lord to show you and give Him your best on the job. He is faithful to help you do great work and to reward you abundantly for your work.

## Personal Reflections/Notes

_____
_____
_____
_____
_____
_____
_____

## Action Steps

_____
_____
_____
_____
_____
_____
_____

# The Woman with the Chronic Illness

## Luke 13:10–16

This woman had been dealing with the same illness for eighteen long years. She had forgotten what it was like to be without pain and to live well and healthy. She could no longer stand up straight nor look people in the eye. She had endured pain, not only from physical affliction but also from loss—loss of gracefulness, capability, relationships, resources, joy, and relevance within her circle of influence. She had been unable to hold her babies or maybe grandbabies. Her desire to hold them was hindered by her severe physical disability. She had lost hope of ever enjoying those small joys until the Master Healer laid His gentle hands on her and set her straight. He restored all that she had lost and given up due to her illness.

Jesus gave her another chance to enjoy those little things and the joys of everyday activities. Now she can laugh out loud again without any pain; she can look forward to picking up those precious babies without wincing in pain. She can go everywhere serving the Lord and proclaiming all that He had done to restore her body, soul, and dignity. Jesus's words to her in Luke 13:12, "Woman, you are loosed from your infirmity," set her free forever from every pain and sickness that had held her doubled over and bound for almost two decades.

It does not matter how long you have been in pain or been held bound by that particular illness or situation. God is not a respecter of persons, and what He has done for others He will do for you in a similar situation. He will honor your faith in Him as you desire to be free from every bondage and shackle of the enemy. Take hold of the word of the Lord and embrace it personally today. Receive His freedom today and walk into the new life that Christ has prepared for you. Put your name in the scripture "——, you are loosed from your infirmity."

## Personal Reflections/Notes

_____

_____

_____

_____

_____

_____

_____

## Action Steps

_____

_____

_____

_____

_____

_____

# Mary, the Mother of Jesus

———— ⤫ ————

Matthew 1:18–25, 12:46–50, 13:55;
Mark 3:31–35; Luke 1:26–38, 39–56,
2:1–7, 15–19, 42–1, 8: 19–21;
John 2:1–12, 19:25–27;
Acts 1:14; Isaiah 7:14

Mary had a divine prophecy hanging over her life. A prophecy that had been declared way before her time, something she probably was unaware of personally. She was not clear about what her exact role in the fulfillment of the prophecy would be. In the fullness of time, as God had determined, Mary stepped forward, in total submission to the God of her fathers. In total surrender, Mary said to the Angel, "be it unto me according to your word" (Luke 1:38).

Mary was an ordinary and obscure young woman whose immediate life goal was to marry Mr. Joseph, the honorable carpenter that her family had approved to be her husband and life partner. While their wedding plans were underway, she had the most bizarre experience that changed her life from ordinary to extraordinary. An angelic visitation that brought with it the news that she was going to have a baby Son before she got married. How could this be since she was a virgin, and she had no intention of violating God's law? However, the Angel assured her that this was going to be a supernatural conception that will not involve Joseph. She would not need to break God's law to have this special baby. Mary was reassured, accepted the message, and gave her consent to be the mother of God's only begotten Son.

Even though Mary was unaware that Isaiah's prophecy was pointing at her, her obedience brought her into God's perfect will for her life—to be the birth mother of Jesus, the Christ, the Messiah, the Anointed One.

Whether you have caught a glimpse of what God has planned for your future or you have received a word of prophecy from His servant, or you currently have no clue about what God has planned for you, your daily obedience to His word in the little things is critical. It will keep you on the path to not only discover God's will for your life; it will bring you into the fullness of the eternal purpose and plan that He has prepared for you. Your next step of obedience might be the very step that brings you into the plan that God has for you. The series of small, inconsequential *obediences* will get you into all that the Father has planned for you. Stay in line with those small steps, and watch God unfold His beautiful plan for your life, just like He did with Mary.

## Personal Reflections/Notes

_____
_____
_____
_____
_____
_____
_____
_____

## Action Steps

_____
_____
_____
_____
_____
_____
_____

# Eve

—— ✺ ——

## Genesis 1:26, 27, 2:18, 21–23, 3:1–20; Isaiah 9:6; 1 Timothy 2:15

She is "now bone of my bones and flesh of my flesh; she shall be called woman." Eve fell from her exalted place with Adam, to a low level where all that she was to Adam was *the mother of all living.* Sin robbed her of her identity. Her real self was lost because of her disobedience to God's commandment. She went from enjoying God's presence to hiding from Him. She also lost the innocence and transparency that she had with her best friend, husband and soul mate, Adam.

How could one wrong move, one wrong conversation, be so monumental in a person's life? For Eve and Adam, there was no going back into the Garden, the place of perfect peace and bliss. Their glorious past was gone forever, and their future looked bleak and devoid of joy. She had no excitement about her future; neither did she have the desire to keep moving forward. Thank God that His great mercy and rich love made a way of escape for them.

In Genesis 3:16, the curse was released on the Earth, bringing great sorrow and pain in childbearing. By God's divine redemptive plan, the same painful process of childbearing that came because of the curse became the same process that would bring great joy and redemption to all of mankind (Adam's seed). Jesus was born of the Virgin Mary, through the process of natural childbearing, to bring mankind out of death to eternal life. What a great and unprecedented turnaround!

No matter how wretched your beginning was or how many wrong turns you've made, God is able to turn things around for you, to ensure that the place of pain becomes the place of joy unspeakable, full of glory! Glory is in your future, not shame. Victory, not defeat! What are you turning over to Him? Don't let your past hold you back. God is able and willing to start your turnaround today, to begin your makeover into a brand-new person! As you let the King of kings into your space, He'll turn your life right round because He's a master at makeovers!

If you've never accepted Jesus into your heart, and you want to do so, pray this prayer:

> Heavenly Father, I come to You in the Name of Jesus. Your Word says, "Whosoever shall call on the name of the Lord shall be saved" (Acts 2:21). I am calling on You. I pray and ask Jesus to come into my heart and be Lord over my life according to Romans 10:9–10: "If you shall confess with your mouth the Lord Jesus, and shall believe in your heart that God has raised him from the dead, you shall be saved. For with the heart man believes unto righteousness; and with the mouth confession is made unto salvation." I do that now. I confess that Jesus is Lord, and I believe in my heart that God raised Him from the dead.

If you have accepted Jesus but you've strayed away, and now want to return to the Lord, pray this prayer:

> Heavenly Father, in Jesus's Name, I make a fresh and strong commitment today to live the life of a born-again child of God. I ask for the grace to give myself to your word totally. I want to follow your guidance through the Holy Spirit who lives on the inside of me. I choose to make

your word the first priority in my life and the final authority for every area of my life. As I dig into your word, I choose to obey what I read and understand, without arguing or looking for alternate sources. Thank you for loving me and for answering my prayer today in Jesus's name.

## Personal Reflections/Notes

_____
_____
_____
_____
_____
_____
_____

# About the Author

Dr. Bukky Ojuola is a board-certified pediatrician who is passionate about nurturing children and encouraging women to discover and live out God's plan and purpose for their lives.

Bukky and Fola have been married for over two decades and are blessed with Tolu and Tosin. Together, they pastor the Redeemed Christian Church of God, The Redeemed Parish in Lynchburg, Virginia. They are committed to developing and discipling others to spiritual maturity through the Word of God.

CPSIA information can be obtained
at www.ICGtesting.com
Printed in the USA
BVHW031430170921
616889BV00002BA/285

9 781638 444442